*Fira
and the
Full Moon*

Fira and the Full Moon

Fira
and the
Full Moon

WRITTEN BY
GAIL HERMAN

ILLUSTRATED BY
THE DISNEY STORYBOOK ARTISTS

HarperCollins *Children's Books*

First published in the USA by Disney Press,
114 Fifth Avenue, New York, New York, 10011-5690.

First published in Great Britain in 2006
by HarperCollins Children's Books.
HarperCollins Children's Books is a division of
HarperCollins Publishers,
77 - 85 Fulham Palace Road, Hammersmith, London, W6 8JB.

The HarperCollins Children's Books website is
www.harpercollinschildrensbooks.co.uk

978-0-00-721399-3
0-00-721399-9

1

Printed and bound in the UK

Visit disneyfairies.com

This book is proudly printed on paper which contains wood
from well managed forests, certified in accordance with
the rules of the Forest Stewardship Council.
For more information about FSC,
please visit www.fsc-uk.org

Mixed Sources
Product group from well-managed
forests and other controlled sources
www.fsc.org Cert no. SW-COC-1806
© 1996 Forest Stewardship Council
FSC

All About Fairies

IF YOU HEAD toward the second star on your right and fly straight on till morning, you'll come to Never Land, a magical island where mermaids play and children never grow up.

When you arrive, you might hear something like the tinkling of little bells. Follow that sound and you'll find Pixie Hollow, the secret heart of Never Land.

A great old maple tree grows in Pixie Hollow, and in it live hundreds of fairies and sparrow men. Some of them can do water magic, others can fly like the wind, and still others can speak to animals. You see, Pixie Hollow is the Never fairies' kingdom, and each fairy who lives there has a special, extraordinary talent.

Not far from the Home Tree, nestled in the branches of a hawthorn, is Mother Dove, the most magical creature of all. She sits on her egg, watching over the fairies, who in turn watch over her. For as long as Mother Dove's egg stays well and whole, no one in Never Land will ever grow old.

Once, Mother Dove's egg *was* broken. But we are not telling the story of the egg here. Now it is time for Fira's tale...

Fira
and the
Full Moon

1

FIRA STUMBLED UP THE STAIRS to her bedroom in the Home Tree. Her wings dragged on the ground. Her fairy glow had dimmed to a faint glimmer.

Fira was a light-talent fairy. Usually, she glowed especially brightly. But that day she felt too tired to use extra light energy. She felt too tired to fly. Too tired to do anything.

She yawned and stretched her arms wide. Fira had been working hard lately. All the light-talent fairies had. It was a busy time of year. The bushes and plants in Pixie Hollow were bursting with berries and seeds. Harvest-talent fairies worked late into the night, gathering the plentiful crops. So the light-talent fairies' special glows were needed more than ever.

There were celebrations and festivals, where light talents put on dazzling light shows and performed shadow-puppet plays. And long after the sun had set each day, Fira and her friends helped light the orchards and gardens as the harvest-talent fairies worked.

Just that day, the fairies had finished the harvesting. Overflowing baskets filled the Home Tree kitchen and pantry. The work was done. Now Fira was looking forward to a long nap.

Finally, Fira reached her room. Kicking off her petal shoes, she flopped facedown on her bed.

The late-afternoon sunlight shone through Fira's bedroom window. Even though she was ready to sleep – *more than ready*, Fira thought – she didn't close her pine-needle blinds. A light-talent fairy always liked to have a little sunshine brightening a room.

Fira slipped under her dandelion-fluff blanket. All around Pixie Hollow, she knew, Never fairies were working and playing. Cooking-talent fairies prepared the evening meal in the Home Tree kitchen. Art-talent fairies painted and sculpted in their studios. Wing-washing talents cleaned fairies' wings. Fairies milked the dairy mice in the dairy barn and herded caterpillars in the field.

Not me, Fira thought. *I'm not doing anything.*

She closed her eyes. Before she had another thought, she fell fast asleep.

Knock! Knock!

Fira flew out of bed, bumping her head on the ceiling.

"What?" she cried. "What is it?"

"I'm sorry, Fira." Spring, a message-talent fairy, poked her head through the open window. "I didn't know you were sleeping. You're needed at the Firefly Thicket."

Fira sat down on her bed. "What's going on?" she asked sleepily.

"I'm not sure. But there's some sort of

4

firefly trouble."

Spring gave an apologetic wave and took off.

"Firefly trouble," Fira repeated. That didn't sound good.

Each night, a group of specially trained fireflies flew around Pixie Hollow. They landed on tiny torches, giving light to the fairies and sparrow men.

These fireflies were Fira's responsibility. She took pride in training them, and training them well. She liked being in charge. But just this once, maybe, she could ask Luna or Iridessa to take over. It would be so nice to keep sleeping.

No, no, no. Fira shook her head. *If you want something done right, you should do it yourself,* she thought. Not that she didn't trust her friends. Of course she did.

But still…

She sighed. If only she could rest a little while longer. Light-talent fairies' glows were weakest when they were tired. Fira hated when her glow was dim. She liked to light up a room. Maybe her short nap had been enough. She stood and gathered her strength.

Then she flew out into the afternoon. Fira slowed as she got close to Havendish Stream. The Firefly Thicket was in a dense, leafy spot along the far bank. Fira darted around a clump of bushes. Then she spied the entrance, a wide opening in the branches.

"Hello?" she called softly. She ducked her head inside. It was always dark back there. That was why the fireflies liked it.

"Moth!"

Moth was Fira's nickname. Other fairies joked that she loved light like a moth loved a candle flame.

"Over here, Moth." Beck, a friend of Fira's, waved her over. Beck was an animal-talent fairy. She could communicate with all the animals in Never Land.

"I'm glad you're here, Fira," said Elixa, a healing-talent fairy. "You need to know what's going on."

Fira gazed around. The fireflies rested fitfully on branches. Their lights flickered dimly. Some didn't light at all.

Beck patted the wings of one firefly. Elixa placed a leaf compress on another.

"They have the no-fire flu," Elixa explained. "They won't be able to light Pixie Hollow tonight."

Fira groaned. It was almost dusk.

Already the light-talent fairies would be hanging glowworm lanterns. But the lanterns were only decoration. The fireflies did the real work of lighting Pixie Hollow. This was trouble, indeed.

Beck went to her side. "I know you're tired from all the harvesting," she said quietly, trying not to disturb the fireflies. "But is there anything you can do?"

Fira straightened her wings. "Of course there's something I can do!"

She would organise all the light-talent fairies. They would need to light the places fireflies usually brightened: gardens, groves, busy sky routes. And the next night a full moon would be out, which meant there would be a dance in the fairy circle. The light-talent fairies would have to light that, too. There was so much work! She had to get going!

With a quick wave good-bye, Fira set off once again. Her mind raced with details. Which fairies would light the fairy-dust mill? Which ones would cover the forest? And who would light the fairy circle?

It was a lot to ask of fairies who were already tired. *It will be all right*, Fira told herself. *We can manage for now. But what if the fireflies are still sick tomorrow?*

2

FIRA DID DOUBLE DUTY that night. She directed light-talent fairies to all corners of the Home Tree. She guided others to locations around Pixie Hollow: the dairy barn, the fairy-dust mill, and the fairy circle, where celebration-setup fairies were preparing for the Fairy Dance.

The next day, Fira slept until midafternoon.

"I can't remember ever sleeping so late!" she said out loud. Usually, she woke with the dawning sun. "But I worked so hard last night. I must have been exhausted," she added.

Fira felt a little dazed. *Maybe some food will help*, she thought. *I hope there are some leftovers from lunch.* She was ravenous!

A few minutes later, she flew into the tearoom. Sunlight streamed through floor-to-ceiling windows. Just looking at the sunshine made Fira feel better. She stood for a moment in a bright spot, drawing strength from a sunbeam.

The large room was empty of fairies. Dining tables stood bare, without any food in sight.

"Looks like I'll have to wait for dinner." Fira sighed. She hadn't had anything to eat since dinner the night before. *Maybe I'll just sit right here*, she thought. *No use leaving and coming back.*

Then she smiled. One by one, other light-talent fairies straggled into the tearoom. They walked slowly, rubbing their eyes.

A cooking-talent fairy stuck her head

out the kitchen door. "They're here!" she announced. "The light-talent fairies are here!" Serving-talent fairies hurried out, carrying trays of steaming hot acorn soup and poppy puff rolls.

"They've been waiting for us!" Luna said. She sat next to Fira. "How nice!"

At a nearby table, Iridessa yawned. Then her mouth stretched into a grin. She sipped the soup happily. "I'm really waking up now!" she exclaimed.

"Me too," Fira agreed. She took a bite of a roll. "Thank you!" she called to the cooking- and serving-talent fairies.

Fira looked around at the other light-talent fairies. They were perking up but still seemed tired. The night before had taken its toll.

"All right," she said. "I've been

thinking about tonight."

"Tonight?" Luna groaned. "I just woke up. Can't we relax for an hour?"

Fira shook her head. "There's too much work to do." She counted on her fingers. "We have to check on the fireflies. We have to figure out new lighting spots. Havendish Stream was much too dark last night. But I have another plan."

"I have a headache just thinking about doing it all again!" Iridessa put in.

"I know it's hard," Fira admitted, "but— "

"Everyone!" Spring, the message-talent fairy, darted into the tearoom. "A laugh is coming. It's almost here!"

A laugh! Fira drew a quick breath. She knew what Spring meant. Everyone did. A baby Clumsy – a human baby – had laughed for the very first time. And the laugh was so strong, so magical, it was coming to Never Land, where it would become a Never fairy.

"There's going to be an arrival!" Luna cried.

Fira couldn't hold in her excitement. She jumped up quickly. An arrival!

And what if the arrival was a light-talent fairy? Another fairy to help light Pixie Hollow! Fira hardly dared to hope. It would be so wonderful.

Of course, there were so many talents. So many fairy groups deserved to have another member. What were the chances?

"Do you know where it's going to land?" she asked Spring.

"In the orchard!" the messenger said over her shoulder. She was already flying off to deliver the news elsewhere.

Fira grabbed Luna's and Iridessa's hands. "Let's go!"

3

AS THE THREE LIGHT-TALENT fairies flew to the orchard, they were joined by more and more fairies. Beck drew up beside Fira. "Moth, have you heard? This laugh is supposed to be special."

"Aren't they all special?" Vidia said snidely. She was always poking her wings into other fairies' business, trying to stir up trouble.

Beck blushed. "Of course."

Prilla appeared beside them, grinning widely. Prilla had an unusual talent. In the blink of an eye, she could travel to the mainland, the world of Clumsies. Fira had seen her do it. She'd get a strange, glassy-eyed look and wouldn't seem to see anything or anyone. Then, all at once, she'd snap back to Pixie Hollow, with tales of the children she had just visited.

"I just saw this baby!" Prilla told the other fairies. "It's the jolliest Clumsy, so happy and always smiling. Everyone's been waiting for her to laugh. She's been saving it, though, for weeks and weeks. But she finally did it! She laughed! It's sure to be something extraordinary!"

"Hmmm," said Vidia as the fairies landed in the orchard. "Then the new arrival must be a fast-flying fairy. Everyone knows we have the most extraordinary talent."

"With you being the most extraordinary of all?" Fira retorted. Oops! She bit her lip. That snippy comment had just slipped out. Fira usually tried to think before she spoke. She tried not to say or do things in such a hurry that they came out wrong. But it wasn't always easy.

Dozens of fairies and sparrow men hovered eagerly in the orchard. Fira waved to Tinker Bell, a pots-and-pans-talent fairy; to Lily, a garden-talent fairy; and to Orren, a mining-talent sparrow man.

It seemed as if every talent had come. And each fairy hoped that this new arrival would belong to his or her talent group.

Then, suddenly, they all felt it: a slight shifting of the air. Everyone stopped. A wavery shimmer floated above their heads.

A murmur went through the crowd. "The laugh! The laugh!"

The laugh hung above the leafy tree branches for a moment. Then it flew down and settled on the soft green grass.

The shimmer burst apart. And there, before them, sat the arrival.

She rose to her feet, quick and sure. The leftover shimmer of laughter fell around her. It turned into her arrival garment, a soft-as-mist dress.

Fira squeezed Luna's hand tightly. This was it! The arrival was going to make her Announcement. She would tell everyone her talent.

"I'm a light-talent fairy." The young fairy spoke loudly and clearly. "My name is Sparkle."

A sigh went through the crowd. Fira hugged Luna and Iridessa. A new light-talent fairy! What luck!

"Fira! Look!" Luna said urgently.

There, above their heads, a second shimmery light hovered in the air.

"Two arrivals!" Fira gasped. She turned to Prilla. "Are they from the same laugh?"

Prilla nodded. "I told you this laugh was amazing."

All around Prilla, fairies and sparrow men whispered excitedly.

The laugh broke apart, and a sparrow man stood before them. He had long golden curls, just like his sister, Sparkle. "My talent is light," he announced. He smoothed a stray hair back into place. "And my name is Helios," he added.

Two light talents! Fira clapped her hands with joy. This was double the luck!

Vidia shook her head. "I'm so happy for you, light-talent fairies," she said. "You need all the help you can get."

Prilla nudged Fira, her eyes shining with wonder. "Look over there!"

Fira gazed into the distance. Then she saw it. A brightening. A soft twinkle. The air pulsed with energy.

Prilla laughed out loud.

Fira thought, *It can't be!*

But it was. The crowd of fairies and sparrow men stood in stunned silence as the laugh exploded in a shower of light. In its place, a young fairy sprawled on the ground. She stretched her wings in an awkward way, knocking into Vidia, who had leaned in for a better look.

"Watch it!" said Vidia, jumping back.

Fira chuckled.

But then the new fairy found her footing and rose. "My name is Glory," she said.

Fira held her breath.

"I am a light-talent fairy!" Glory

told them.

A cheer rose through the crowd. Luna and Iridessa danced with joy. Fira stood for a moment, not moving. Three arrivals, all light talents. This was truly unheard of.

Vidia flapped her wings and took off. "Three young fairies to train," she called out to Fira. "Triplets! I don't envy you one bit."

Fira laughed. She didn't believe that for a second.

The triplets stood close together. They gazed around, taking in everything.

"Just look at them!" Fira told her friends. "They're so well behaved."

They weren't trying to fly before they were able. They weren't testing their new wings.

Fira remembered her own arrival. She

hadn't been able to stop spinning around and around, fluttering her wings. She kept trying to get off the ground before she even had her magic.

Terence, a dust-talent sparrow man, flew over to the triplets. He sprinkled a teacup of fairy dust on each one.

That will do it, thought Fira. *They have their magic now!*

The triplets began to glow lemon yellow, edged with gold.

"Their glows are very bright," Prilla said.

"And strong, too," added Beck. It was good fairy manners to compliment the new arrivals.

Still, the young fairies didn't move. The crowd whispered, growing nervous. But Fira grinned. They were taking their time, being careful with their magic. *Good for them,* she thought. They were thinking things through.

Then, with a whoop, the three fairies shot high into the air. Everyone cheered. The triplets zipped. They zoomed. They somersaulted and cartwheeled.

The cheers faded as the triplets flew faster and faster, chasing each other. *"I'm flying here. You go over there!"* Sparkle ordered the other two.

She darted into the leaves of a goldenrod plant. "But, Sparkle!" Helios followed her. "I want to play in the flowers, too. See how they match my hair?"

Glory trailed behind, her flying bumpy and uneven. Helios and Sparkle laughed. "Look at the baby. She can't keep up!" they teased.

Glory burst into tears. She wailed so loudly, Beck clapped her hands over her ears.

Then all three fairies were pushing and bumping one another, yelling as loudly as they could.

"What a racket!" said Prilla.

"Uh-oh," Fira murmured.

The triplets were out of control.

The crowd of fairies and sparrow men broke up. Some went over to Fira and the other light-talent fairies. They shook their heads with pity and patted them on the back. A few said, "Congratulations." But Fira thought they really meant "Good luck."

If somebody didn't do something, the triplets would be fighting all day. Fira took a deep breath. She tried to smile at Luna and Iridessa. She would take charge. "I'll bring them to the Home Tree and show them around," she offered.

The other light-talent fairies nodded quickly. "Let us know if you need any help," said Luna. She hurried off with Iridessa.

"I will," Fira said, but they were already too far away to hear.

She turned to the triplets. "I'm Fira," she told them. "I'll take you to your rooms."

"Fly with you!" they cried in unison, offering the fairy greeting. They crowded around Fira. Each one tried to get closer than the others.

"This way," Fira said. She squeezed between Sparkle and Helios. Rising into the air, she set out toward the Home Tree.

She smiled at the arrivals flying beside her. They'd be such a help to the light talents. Sure, they seemed a bit wild. But it was nothing she couldn't manage.

Fira felt sure of it.

IN THE HOME TREE, Fira and the triplets looked at the directory in the lobby. "Here you are," said Fira. "Your room is on the fourth floor."

"*Room?*" Helios repeated. "Does that mean there's only one?"

"We have to share?" asked Sparkle.

"All three of us?" Glory squealed in dismay.

"It's only until the decoration-talent fairies can get two more rooms ready," said Fira. "Besides, it'll be fun. You'll be right next door to me."

They flew together to the triplets' room. Fira opened the door, and the three young fairies crowded inside.

The decoration-talent fairies had been

busy. One moon-shaped fan hung from the ceiling. But Fira noted that there were three of everything else: three beds, stacked one on top of the other. Three walnut-shell dressers with star-shaped knobs. Three mirrors in a row. Each reflected light from a different window, and each one was larger than the next.

"Here we are!" Fira said.

"I get the top bunk!" Sparkle called.

"No, I want the top one!" said Helios.

"No, me!" cried little Glory.

But Sparkle was already sitting on the bed, swinging her legs. "I'm oldest. I choose first."

"All right," grumbled Helios. "You can have it. But the mirror closest to the light is mine." He stopped to admire himself.

"I wanted that one!" Glory whined.

She spun around. "But I'm going to choose a dresser first." She raced to the dresser in the far corner.

"Ha-ha," Sparkle teased, flying faster. "Beat you!" She pulled open a drawer.

"Not fair!" screamed Glory. She caught sight of the biggest window. "I'll open the shade," she declared.

"No, me," said Helios. He darted forward.

"I want to," Sparkle called out.

All three dashed toward the window at once.

"Hold on!" Fira stepped in front of them. "I'll get it."

She snapped the shade open.

"I'll get the other ones!" said Sparkle.

"No, wait!" Fira said. She wanted their crazy contest to end. "Look outside. There are the mining-talent fairies."

Fira pointed out the window, to the roots of the Home Tree. In a shady corner, two mining-talent fairies were cleaning their tools.

"Let me see!" Sparkle rushed to the window.

"Me too!" Helios flew next to her. Glory tried to squeeze in between them. Giving up, she fluttered up and down, looking over their heads.

"What strange fairies!" exclaimed Helios.

"They just look a little different from the other fairies," Fira explained. "Because mining work needs less flying than other talents, their wings are smaller. And mining-talent fairies are usually shorter, closer to the ground. So they're are more comfortable in the mines."

"And their clothes!" Helios said. He smoothed his arrival garment, which was brand-new and brightly coloured. "They look like rags!"

"Not quite like rags," Fira scolded, a little sharply. "They must be getting ready to go mining. And why wear your best clothes if you'll be covered in dust and dirt?" She turned back to the window and leaned out partway.

"Hello, Precious! Hello, Orren!" Fira called down.

The fairies shaded their eyes and looked up at the window. Neither one smiled.

"Are you going on an expedition?" Fira asked.

"Of course we're going," Precious

replied.

"There's a full moon tonight," Orren said grumpily.

Sparkle tapped Fira on the shoulder. "Why don't they sound more excited?"

"Well, that's just their way," Fira said. She wasn't really paying attention. The mining-talent fairies had reminded her of the firefly flu. Usually, the fireflies settled on miners' helmets to light the tunnels. Would they be well enough to help by that night?

She leaned out again to explain the problem to the miners. "I'm not sure any light talents will be able to guide you. We may need to light Pixie Hollow. Maybe you should hold off," she finished.

"Wait a day."

"Hold off?" Precious scowled. "Wait a

day? But we always go on the night of the full moon. Always."

"She thinks our work can wait," Orren grumbled. "She thinks that Pixie Hollow doesn't need iron or metal. No, no, no." He shook his head. "Don't mind us. We're just mining-talent fairies. Not important at all. Not like other talents."

"I don't think that," Fira hastened to call down. "I'm – "

A loud crash sounded behind her. Fira spun around. A shattered vase lay on the floor. Miniature sunflowers were strewn among the pieces. Water seeped everywhere.

"Glory did it!" said Sparkle.

"Helios did it," said Glory.

"Sparkle did it," said Helios.

"It doesn't matter who did it," Fira

said. "You need to be more careful."

She helped the triplets clean up the mess. Firefly trouble or no firefly trouble, she had to get these young fairies outside. They needed to use up some energy.

"Come on!" she told them. "I'm giving you a tour of Pixie Hollow!"

Fira and the triplets hovered just outside the Home Tree. *Where should we begin?* Fira wondered. *What would keep them interested?*

"Moth!" Tinker Bell flew out of her workshop. The shop was really an old Clumsy teakettle. Tink had magically transported it to the Home Tree and squeezed it inside. Its door stood under a steel awning, which was actually the spout turned upside down.

"I was just coming to get you!" Tinker Bell said. "I've come up with a new teakettle for you. It has a few surprises I think you'll like."

Fira grinned. She loved to drink tea in her room each morning while watching the sun rise. *What could this new kettle do that any old one couldn't?* she wondered.

"Come inside!" Tink told her.

Fira glanced at the triplets. Maybe it wasn't a good idea to bring them inside quite yet.

Tink caught her look. "Are the triplets giving you any trouble?" she asked.

"Not a bit." Fira tossed her head. She didn't want Tink to think that three brand-new fairies were getting the best of her.

"Let's go, Sparkle, Helios, Glory!" she called. "Here's the first stop of our tour!"

"Why do you always call Sparkle first?" Helios demanded. "Do you like her best?"

"Why do you always call me last?" Glory said tearfully.

They kept arguing as they trailed Fira and Tinker Bell inside. "Not one bit of trouble?" Tink asked.

Fira laughed. "Well, all right. I'll admit it. Maybe just a bit."

It wasn't just the arrivals that troubled her, of course. It was all that light-talent planning… and the miners' expedition… and the fireflies. Fira really had a lot going on.

Not too much, she told herself. *Just a lot.*

Tink and Fira flew to a corner of the shop. Fira's kettle sat on a worktable, next to a pile of dented trays.

"Is it okay if the triplets take a look around?" Fira asked Tinker Bell.

Tinker Bell frowned, then nodded. "Just don't touch anything," she told the young fairies.

She turned back to Fira and put the kettle over the fire. "When the tea is ready," Tink explained, "steam comes out the spout in different colours."

"Really?" Fira peered at the kettle. It looked exactly the same as any old teakettle. But with Tink's pots-and-pans magic, you never knew what could happen.

Across the room, Sparkle picked up a small frying pan. "Tink said no touching!" Glory reminded her.

Sparkle dropped the pan quickly. It clanged on the ground.

"But what's this?" Sparkle pointed to a drawing on the handle. It was a tiny pot with squiggly lines for steam rising from it.

"That's my talent mark," Tink told her. "See my initials? T.B.?"

The triplets crowded around. They squinted to see the letters. "Oh, yes!" said Helios. He looked around. "This strainer has your talent mark, too."

"And each piece in this silverware set!" added Glory.

The triplets twisted and turned, checking under handles and inside pots. They were careful not to touch a thing.

Fira smiled. They really were trying.

"Can you show me how this kettle works?" she asked Tinker Bell.

Tink nodded and said, "When the tea is ready, the kettle whistles and steam comes out, just like always. But the steam is coloured. And each colour is for a different kind of tea. Watch this now."

Just then, the teakettle whistled. A bright orange cloud came out of the spout. "Orange is for thirst-quenching tea," Tink explained.

The colour changed to bright red. "A fiery red steam is for early-morning, just-waking-up tea."

Next, the steam turned a light shade of blue. "And soothing baby blue is perfect for a nighttime cup of tea."

While Tink was talking, Fira sneaked glances at the triplets. Their backs were bent over a worktable. They seemed to be studying a big metal sheet. Fira couldn't see much. But they were quiet. They weren't arguing or knocking things over.

They were fine.

"Would you care for a nice cup of orange tea?" Tink asked. The steam changed back to orange. She cleared a space at a table and poured two cups. The friends sat down together.

Fira took a sip. "Mmmm! Delicious!"

Tink wrinkled her nose.

"You don't like it?" asked Fira.

Tinker Bell shook her head. "It's not that. Do you smell a funny odour?"

Fira sniffed. There was a definite burning smell in the workshop. What could it be?

The triplets!

At the very same moment, Fira and Tinker Bell turned to the triplets. A cloud of black smoke enveloped them.

In a flash, Fira raced over. "Are you

okay?" she yelled, waving away the smoke.

"We're fine," Sparkle said in a quiet voice.

Tink let out a little shriek. "But my brand-new triple-shine copper isn't!" she wailed. She held out the sheet. A giant hole had been burned right through its center.

"Um, um," Helios stuttered. "We were making sparks… "

He snapped his fingers to show Tink. A bright spark flew from his fingertips.

"To try to burn our own talent marks," Sparkle went on, "and – "

"And we got a little carried away." Glory hung her head.

"The metal is ruined!" Fira was horrified. How could they have been so careless? "I'd fly backward if I could," she told Tinker Bell, apologising in the fairy way. "I feel responsible."

But Tinker Bell barely heard. She moved the sheet this way and that. She tugged on her bangs, deep in thought.

"All I have to do is thin this piece out here… bring the extra metal there… ," Tink said, already lost in her repair job. She was too caught up in fixing the sheet to even tell Fira that everything was all right.

"I'd fly backward, too," Sparkle said.

"I'd fly further," Helios said.

"No, me! I'd fly backward furthest," Glory shouted.

"Shhh! Let's leave Tinker Bell to her work." Fira pushed the noisy triplets out the door.

They were back where they had

started, outside the Home Tree. Fira ran her hands through her hair. Now what in Never Land could she do with them?

5

THE THREE YOUNG FAIRIES clustered around Fira. They peppered her with questions and demands.

"What should we do next, Fira?"

"Where can we go?"

"I want to see mermaids."

"I want to visit Tinker Bell again."

"I want to go to the fairy-dust mill!"

"Stop!" Fira practically shouted. She took a deep breath. "I'll tell you where we'll go."

It was a hard decision. Tink had been a good sport about the mishap in her workshop. In fact, she seemed happy to have a problem to fix. Still, Fira would have to think carefully before she brought the triplets anywhere else.

What would be a nice, quiet place? A soothing place, where everyone could relax?

A garden! Fira decided. One with sweet-smelling flowers, shady nooks, and pretty plants. And why not take them to her favorite garden in all of Pixie Hollow? Lily's garden.

"I know just the place," Fira told them. "This way."

She led the triplets past the Home Tree. They flew over a hedge of raspberry bushes. And there was Lily's garden.

A blanket of sweet clover covered the ground. Rows of lilacs and Queen Anne's lace stood in shady groves. The triplets stared. For once, they were speechless.

Fira grinned. She'd made the right choice! Then she spied Lily standing by a young flower.

"You can do it!" Lily whispered to the flower. "You can grow big and strong."

"Wow!" said Fira quietly. She flew closer. "I've never seen that kind of poppy before."

Lily smiled. "It's my first blue poppy! It's doing great. It just needs a little encouragement." She turned to smile at the triplets. "New visitors! Fly with you."

"I'm showing them around Never Land," Fira explained. "And of course we had to stop here."

"Come," Lily said. "You can see my wild rose... and my Queen Anne's lace ... and my... "

Fira sat in the shade of a daffodil while Lily led the triplets to each grove and patch of grass. The young fairies were busy. That was good. Fira could take a break and turn her attention to other problems. The fireflies and their flu, to start with.

It was getting late in the day, and the sun was low in the sky. What if the fireflies still weren't feeling any better? The mining-talent fairies would be setting off in just a few hours. They'd need light.

Fira figured she should check with Elixa, the healing-talent fairy. Maybe she'd had some luck finding a cure for the flu.

Wait! Fira sat up straight. Lily's garden had all sorts of herbs and special plants. They could be used for medicine! Were the fireflies trying any of those?

"Lily!" Fira called. She flew over to a wild rosebush. The triplets were measuring their wingspans against a petal.

"My wings are almost twice the size of

a rose petal!" Sparkle said proudly.

"Well, my wings are, too," Helios declared. "And just as soft."

"How about me? How about me?" Glory hopped up and down.

"Have you heard about the firefly flu?" Fira asked Lily above their voices. "Has anyone been here to pick plants for a healing potion?"

Lily nodded. "I've been away on a seed hunt. But Elixa came while I was gone. She left a note saying that she took some herbs. She could be using them for the fireflies."

"Really?" Fira brightened. "Can you show me?"

The two fairies flew off. "Stay there," Fira shouted back to the triplets. "We'll be right back."

Lily took Fira to the far corner of the

garden. They landed in a sunny grassy patch. "Elixa chose mint leaves from right here," Lily said.

Fira studied the plant. She didn't know much about mint, but maybe it would do some good. "How much – " she began. Then she realised that Lily's face had turned ashen.

"What is it?" Fira asked, panicked. "What's wrong?"

"I'm not sure," Lily said. "One of my flowers is upset. I can feel it." She closed her eyes. "It's… it's… it's my brand-new poppy!"

Lily rushed away, with Fira close behind. "This has nothing to do with the triplets." Fira tried to convince herself. "They wouldn't hurt a flower!"

But then she saw the three young fairies

by Lily's new blue poppy. They were glowing their brightest.

"We're having a contest," Helios said, "to see whose glow the flower likes best."

His glow grew brighter. The poppy stretched toward his light, as it would toward the sun.

"Ha!" said Sparkle. "My glow is stronger." She blazed with light. The poppy leaned away from Helios and toward her.

"No fair!" said Glory. "You two are bigger!" She frowned in concentration. She began to glitter and shimmer. The flower twisted in her direction.

"Stop!" Lily cried. "The poppy is exhausted! Please leave it alone."

"Dim your glows," Fira commanded.

The daylight seemed to darken as the triplets obeyed. Lily hovered by the poppy.

"There, there," she said soothingly. "It's all over. You'll be right as rain in a few minutes."

"Did we do something wrong?" Glory asked, confused.

"We? Maybe it was just you!" said Sparkle. "You went last!"

Glory began to cry.

"I'd fly backward, Lily," Fira apologised. "I should have been watching them more carefully."

"It will be all right." Lily spoke in that same cooing voice. But this time, she was looking at Fira.

"Come on. Let's go," Fira told the triplets, "before we do any more harm."

They left Lily still tending her poppy. Fira fluttered her wings, unsure of what to do next. She really needed to check on the fireflies. But what about the triplets?

The three fairies looked at Fira hopefully. Fira sighed. The Pixie Hollow tour wasn't working out anyway. She should take the triplets back to their room. And while she was at the Home Tree, she could stop and see Elixa in her potions workshop. Maybe Elixa had some good news.

"All right," said Fira. "I'm taking you home."

"Why? What are you doing now?" Sparkle asked. "Are you going to your room, too?"

"Uh, no. I have some business."

"Light-talent business?"

"Can we go, too?"

"Can we? Can we?"

The sun was beginning to set. The

mining expedition would be leaving in just a little while. It would take too long to argue with the triplets. It would be faster to let them tag along.

"Okay," Fira said. "But this time, stay out of trouble!"

6

THE POTIONS WORKSHOP was on the third floor of the Home Tree. The door was wide open.

Fira knocked. Then she flew in, followed by the triplets.

The young fairies gazed around the room. Rows of birch-bark shelves filled the workshop from ceiling to floor. Each shelf was crammed with potions, medicines, and plant extracts. Each jar was clearly labeled.

"'Ground-up pine nuts,'" Sparkle read. "'Laurel-leaf bits.' 'Sesame oil.'"

"Elixa?" Fira called. She flew up and down the rows.

"Let's open the jars and smell what's inside," Sparkle whispered to the others.

She twisted off a top. "Ugh! Peat moss."

Glory and Helios started to open jars, too.

"Don't do that," Fira warned, flying back.

"'Right-on-thyme powder. Very fine,'" Helios read, flying to a top shelf.

Sparkle picked up the jar. "Glory, you should try this!" she called. "You're always last. You're never on time." She pretended to toss it to the younger fairy.

"Stop!" Fira hissed. She took the jar out of Sparkle's hands and put it back on the shelf.

"Is there any skin cream here, I wonder?" Helios said as he sorted through more potions in a corner.

"This is a workshop," Fira said. "We really have to be careful."

"Okay," Glory agreed. She spun around clumsily, knocking over a jug marked MUSHROOM POISON! STAY AWAY!

Fira caught the bottle just before it hit the ground.

"Elixa?" she called loudly, and a bit desperately. "Are you here?"

"Yes!"

Fira jumped. Elixa had stepped out from behind a potted miniature raindrop cactus. She wore a light green smock, with lots of big deep pockets, and long gloves.

"I didn't mean to scare you," Elixa said. She smiled at the triplets. "I was so busy working. I didn't realize you were here."

Elixa held up a tube made from a plant stem. One end was stuck into the prickly cactus. "I'm extracting cactus juice."

"Is this part of a potion for the firefly flu?" Fira asked. "Along with the plants from Lily's garden?"

Elixa nodded. "I'm going to mix this with some ground-up mint. It should be an equal blend. One part soothing herb. One part sharp cactus medicine that gets right to the point of healing. Come look."

Fira hesitated. "Oh, the triplets will be fine," Elixa said, as if reading her mind.

Fira wasn't so sure. But she really wanted to examine the healing potion. "Stay still," she ordered the triplets.

She ducked behind the cactus with Elixa. They both sat down, and Fira sighed. It felt good to rest. "See? Here comes the juice now," Elixa said. "I'll just give a careful squeeze to this part of the cactus. There!"

"When will it be ready?" Fira asked.

"Oh, not too long now," Elixa said. "Maybe another hour."

"Another hour? You mean the fireflies will be better soon? They can light Pixie Hollow tonight? And go on the mining expedition?"

Fira felt a burst of energy. Her glow flared. Things were beginning to look up.

Elixa sat back on her heels. She carefully placed the healing potion on a worktable. "Well, the fireflies can take the medicine right after it's finished. But I'm not sure how long it will take to work. It might be a few hours. It might be a few days."

"But tonight is the full moon! The expedition leaves no matter what."

Boom! The cactus gave a sudden jerk.

Its spines shook. The plant stretched higher. It was growing!

"What's going on?" Elixa darted around, unsure of what to do.

With another jerk, the cactus grew a bit more.

"The triplets!" Fira said. She raced around the plant to find the three fairies.

Silently, Glory held out an open jar. "'Growing powder,'" Fira read.

"I wanted to grow," Glory admitted. "But I dropped some onto the cactus by accident."

"Silly little fairy," said Sparkle. She reached for the jar.

"Maybe it will work on my hair," said Helios, reaching, too.

As Glory pulled back, the others leaned forward. The jar tipped over. The rest of the powder poured onto the cactus.

The plant shot up, knocking over jars and shelves. Its sharp spines scraped the walls. Fira grabbed the healing potion from the worktable just before a fast-growing spine knocked it over.

Fira flew toward the ceiling, trying to outrace the growing cactus. The cactus stretched toward her. The workshop shook with the force.

"I can't go any higher!" Fira cried when she reached the ceiling.

Afraid, the triplets pressed themselves against the wall. But the cactus spines kept coming... closer, and closer still, as the plant grew.

"We're going to get poked!" Glory shouted. "We can't escape."

The fairies squeezed themselves into a

corner. Glory gasped as a cactus spine pricked her clothes.

"Stay calm," Elixa ordered. She reached into a pocket of her smock and took out a small potions kit. "I always keep an emergency stash handy," she said.

She quickly mixed some green and red powders together. Then she soared between the needles, sprinkling the powder over the cactus.

The plant jerked again. Then, slowly, it began to shrink.

"Whew," said Elixa. "That was close."

Fira helped the triplets out of the corner. But the laboratory was a disaster. Broken jars littered the floor. A layer of spilled powder covered tables, chairs, and shelves. Cactus spines stuck out of seat cushions and through potion recipe books.

Everything was in shambles – again!

"We'll help clean up," Sparkle offered. "Right, you two?" she said to the others.

Glory and Helios nodded. "Do you have any extra smocks?" Helios asked. "I don't want to get my clothes dirty."

Elixa shook her head. "I think you're better off leaving things alone. This is a delicate job. Potions might get mixed together, and that could be trouble. Really, only healing-talent fairies should help."

"I'd fly backward," Fira said for what felt like the millionth time that day.

Elixa shrugged. "That's okay."

Fira held up the healing potion for the fireflies. "At least we still have this."

Elixa eyed the triplets, then took the jar. "I'd better hold on to it."

Fira agreed. "We'll leave now," she said. She turned to the triplets.

But they were already gone.

7

THOSE FAIRIES! FIRA THOUGHT. *First Tink's metal. Then Lily's flower. Then the mess at Elixa's workshop. And now they've flown off without a word. Who knows where they could have gone?*

She tried to think calmly. But her mind was racing. Sparkle had wanted to see the Mermaid Lagoon. Fira would start there.

But only the mermaids were at the lagoon, singing mermaid songs and combing their hair.

Next, Fira visited the fairy-dust mill, the dairy barn, and Havendish Stream. The triplets were nowhere to be found.

It was getting dark now. Not knowing what to do, Fira flew home. Her wings felt heavy. She yawned.

Finally, she flew into the first floor of the Home Tree. Up she went through the holes in the ceilings, climbing floor by floor. She knew she had lots to think about. The triplets still needed to be found. And then there were the fireflies. What would happen to Pixie Hollow and the mining-talent fairies if the fireflies still had the flu? Fira needed to make some plans.

But right now, all she wanted was to lie on her bed, close her eyes, and rest.

She flew past the triplets' room.

Soft sounds escaped through the keyhole. Fira stopped short. They'd been there all along! If only she hadn't been so hasty. If only she hadn't wasted time scouring Pixie Hollow from one end to the other. She could have been napping instead. Of course she should have tried their room first.

She burst into the bedroom.

The three sat close together on one bed. They looked up, happy to see Fira. "You're here!" said Sparkle. "We've been waiting for you!"

"We made such a mess of things. We didn't want to go anywhere else," Helios explained.

"What can we do to make things better?" Glory asked.

Was there anything they could do? Fira hesitated.

Just then, Spring, the message-talent fairy, flew in behind her. "I have a message from Elixa," Spring told Fira. "The fireflies are feeling better."

"Thank goodness!" Fira clapped

her hands.

"But their glow is still weak," Spring went on. "They might not be able to light Pixie Hollow for the whole night."

Fira drooped. Once again, the light-talent fairies couldn't rest. Just in case the fireflies lost their glow, the fairies had to be ready to fill in.

"The fireflies can't guide the miners, either," continued Spring. "It's too risky."

No fireflies on the expedition? No light-talent fairies who could leave Pixie Hollow?

That left Fira – and Fira alone – to lead the miners.

An hour later, Fira sat in her room. She gazed at the full moon, drawing strength from its light. She'd already helped the light-talent fairies find their places around

Pixie Hollow. She'd even made a schedule for them. Now it was almost time for the expedition.

Fira knew she was taking on a lot. After all the flying and chasing and fairy-sitting she'd done that day, she felt tired already. But she had to be strong. She was in charge. And so many fairies were counting on her.

She got up to leave.

Knock, knock, knock.

"No fair." Sparkle's voice came through the door loud and clear. "I told you I'd knock first."

"But you always go first," Glory complained. "Why can't I knock first?"

Helios said, "Knock, snock. Let's just go in. I'm sure Fira will be glad to see us. Are my wings straight?"

Fira opened the door. "I was just on my way out," she told them.

"We need to say something first," said Sparkle. She stepped in front of the others.

Fira glanced at the moon. Time was running out. "I know you feel bad about everything that happened," she said to the triplets. She tried not to sound impatient. "You've told me already. But I really need to go. The miners need me."

"We know. We want you to take us with you," Sparkle said. "We can help."

"Yes!" said Helios. "You didn't give us an assignment for tonight. All the other light-talent fairies have one."

"You don't trust us," added Glory, "because we made such a mess of things." She jumped up and down and hit her head against the doorframe. "Ouch! But we have lots of light energy. We can really help... if you'll let us."

Fira stared at the triplets. For a moment, she thought maybe they could help her with the mining trip. But then she remembered everything that had happened. Of course they were too young and too inexperienced to go.

"The best way for you to help is to stay in your room," she told them. "Don't go anywhere. Don't do anything. Don't even talk to anyone."

Without another word, she darted out the window. As she flew, she could hear the triplets.

"This is all your fault, Glory."

"No, it's not. It's your fault, Sparkle. You're always so bossy."

"What about Helios? He never pays attention. Stop looking in that mirror, Helios!"

But soon their voices faded away. Fira flew on, alone.

8

THE NEVER MINE WAS DEEP in the woods. The entrance was a cave in a small clearing.

Fira flew there quickly. She soared through the night in the light of the full moon.

Outside the mine, Precious, Orren, and the other miners waited. One mouse stood ready, a mining cart harnessed to his back. The cart was empty. But the miners hoped to fill it with Never iron, pewter, and other metals. Another mouse carried sacks filled with axes, shovels, and picks.

Fira landed next to Orren. "I'm here," she said, "ready to light the tunnel."

Just then, a large cloud covered the moon. The woods darkened, and Fira shivered.

"All right, Fira. It's time to go," Orren said in his gloomy voice. "Everyone, form a line. Fira, you should go first."

One by one, the fairies, sparrow men, and mice entered the tunnel. Fira brightened her glow. The tunnel was wide, but its ceiling was low, so the fairies had to walk instead of flying.

By the light of her own glow, Fira could see bits of wood shoring up the cave ceiling. Clouds of dust danced around her feet. The miners plodded through the tunnel with heavy steps.

"We'll need to go far into the cave," Precious said from behind Fira. "All the ore has been mined near the front."

Still, the mining expedition continued at the same slow pace. The fairies crept like snails through the tunnel. Bit by bit, the path narrowed. It dipped deep underground. It twisted and turned, splitting in two again and again.

"Left," Orren directed Fira. "Now right. Take that tunnel. The one with the steep stairs."

This is more complicated than any maze, Fira thought. *I'm glad Orren knows the way!*

Not one glimmer of light seeped into the mine from outside now. The air felt cool.

They went farther and farther into the tunnel. Water dripped from the walls. Fira hugged herself for warmth and turned up her glow.

Her step was slowing. Her bones felt weary. She was glad when Orren said, "Stop. I have to check the map."

She rested a moment, directing her

glow so that Orren could read. "We're almost there," he said. "Crystal Cave is just ahead. Past there, we should find new ore."

Orren squinted. "Can you glow a bit more brightly?" he asked Fira. "Everyone needs to be able to see."

Fira concentrated. Her light blazed more strongly.

"Thank you," Orren said gruffly.

A few moments later, they stepped into a large cavern. Fira spun slowly. Glittering gems lined the walls. They reflected Fira's light with brilliant reds, greens, and blues. Fira felt refreshed, as if her wings had been washed with cool water on a hot summer day. Her glow brightened.

"Beautiful, isn't it?" Precious said. Her voice sounded lighter to Fira. Almost happy.

Precious reached out and touched one of the gems. Fira could tell that Precious loved these rocks, just as Fira loved light. They were her joy. Fira gave Precious an understanding smile. Precious smiled back. Then she added in her gloomy way, "But we need to keep moving."

The expedition trudged forward. "Here it is," announced Orren. Fira stopped. They stood in another large opening. But this cavern had no jewels. Its walls were smooth and bare.

"We can begin," Orren told the others. Each miner took a tool.

Fira sat in the centre of the chamber. She cast her light into one corner, then another. She tried to brighten each spot in the cavern.

If they mine as slowly as they walk, Fira

thought, *we'll be here until the next full moon.*

But the miners were as quick as lightning. They struck the walls with picks. They hacked away at stones with axes. They shoveled bits of ore into the mouse cart.

"Try this area!" Precious directed. "Go deeper over there!"

Fira drew on all her strength to keep the room lit.

In just a little while, the cart was filled. "Our job is done," Orren said. "We can go."

The group started retracing their steps. Fira slipped on a stone and faltered. She righted herself. But something was wrong. Her glow was dimming. Full moon or no full moon, she felt more tired than she'd ever felt before.

I can't keep up my glow, she thought.

After a few more steps, they entered Crystal Cave. Fira hoped that the bright gems would help her once again.

Whoosh! A sharp gust of wind blew through the cavern. It hit Fira full force. She shook with the chill.

"Oh, no!" she moaned. Her glow flickered, then went out.

The jewels shone dimly. Fira guessed that the gems were picking up bits of light from the low, dim glows of the miners.

"Too dark," said Orren. "Can't make out much of anything."

"Not even the way out," Precious said with a shrug.

"We can't leave Crystal Cave!" Fira cried. "We can't go anywhere at all!"

They were trapped!

9

"UH-HUH," ORREN AGREED with Fira. "We're stuck, all right."

"Looks like we're goners," Precious added in a flat tone.

The other miners shuffled their feet. Some sat, leaning against big rocks. One miner twiddled her thumbs. Another scratched an itch.

Orren poured cups of water for everyone from a chestnut-shell canteen.

Nobody panicked. Nobody cried out in fear. They settled on the ground and accepted their fate. Even the mice stood quietly.

"I'm not giving up!" Fira said.

But what could she do? They were so

far underground. So far from light.

The only thing she could do was rest… and see if her glow came back.

She found a corner where the gems twinkled the most brightly. Sitting back against the wall, she closed her eyes.

A heaviness settled over her wings. She felt herself drift. Seconds passed, then minutes. Finally, Fira sat up with a start. Had she even slept? She didn't think so. She was too anxious.

"Feeling better?" Orren asked.

Fira wasn't sure. A blast of cool air blew through the cavern. She shivered. She hadn't felt cold when the expedition had kept moving. But now that they were staying in one spot, she felt chilled to the bone. Her stomach rumbled with hunger.

"I'll try to glow now," she told Orren.

Fira took a deep breath. Her glow flickered, strong and bright. She grinned. It was working! But then, as if a switch had turned it off, the light snuffed out.

Fira took another breath and tried with every inch of her being to glow.

Nothing happened.

"This is all my fault!" she cried. "We're trapped here because of me."

Orren patted her back. "There, there. We knew the danger. We wanted to go. We are at fault."

Fira knew that it was useless to place blame. But she couldn't help scolding herself.

"Oh, why did I come on my own?" she asked herself aloud. "I could have taken another light talent or two. But no, no. I was so sure I could do this alone, without anyone's help. And now we're all in real trouble." She put her head in her hands.

"There, there," Orren said again, awkwardly. "Someone will come looking for us. Eventually."

"Eventually." Fira sighed. How long would that be?

Fira and the miners fell quiet. In the silence, Fira heard a noise. It sounded like a giggle.

Was she imagining things?

Tee-hee.

It *was* a giggle!

"What?" A few miners raised their heads.

"Shhh!" Fira held a finger to her lips. Now she heard voices. Three different voices, talking to one another. Arguing.

Could it be?

The voices grew louder.

"I see footprints over here!"

"No! There are more footprints this way. Let's take this tunnel."

"No, no, no, Sparkle. You think you know everything. This is the way to go!"

It was the triplets! They were right outside Crystal Cave!

"Sparkle! Helios! Glory!" shouted Fira. She had never thought she'd be so happy to hear their arguing.

"Helios! Glory! Sparkle!" she added, to be fair. Then, "Glory, Sparkle, Helios! We're here! We're here!"

10

THE TRIPLETS BURST INTO Crystal Cave. Their glows lit the room with a dazzling brightness.

Fira rushed over to give them hugs. "What are you doing here?" she cried.

Sparkle shrugged. For once, she seemed unsure. "We thought we could help."

"We know we didn't listen to you," Helios added. "You told us to stay in our room. But we followed you. We thought you might have trouble. We thought you really could use our help."

"Yes," Glory put in. "We all agreed. We didn't have one fight about it."

"Our glows are so strong," Sparkle said. "We have all this energy. And you seemed... tired."

Precious stepped closer. "Looks like we're rescued," she said with a sigh.

"Yes," said Orren. "Let's give a cheer."

"Hooray," the miners chimed together in flat voices. "Hooray for the triplets."

"Well, what are we waiting for?" Fira laughed with relief. "Let's get going!"
This time, the triplets led the way. They took turns going first, the other two walking behind with Fira.

"So you're not angry?" Glory asked.

Fira shook her head. "You really rescued us. I should have realized what a help you'd be. I judged you too quickly."

And wasn't I just as rash when I was a young fairy? Fira thought. Even now, she didn't always think everything through. Like the triplets, she was still learning. *After all, a true leader has to work as part of a team.*

The expedition wound its way back through the maze of tunnels. Then, as the sun began to rise, they went out of the cave entrance and into the woods.

"Not much longer now," said Precious in a glum voice. "We're almost home."

A few minutes later, the miners stopped at the dairy barn. "We have to put these mice to bed now," Orren said. "So we'll part here."

Fira hugged Precious. The mining fairy stood stiffly for a moment. Then Fira felt her hug back. "See you in the tearoom!" Fira called to the miners.

But suddenly, she let out a jaw-cracking yawn. She felt too tired for breakfast. Instead, the triplets led her to her cosy room.

"Here," said Helios. He passed by the mirror without so much as a glance. "You get into bed."

"Yes," Sparkle agreed. "Good idea, Helios." She took Fira's shoes off and fluffed up the pillow. Fira lay down. Glory pulled the blanket up to her chin.

"Hey!" said Fira sleepily. "You're still not fighting."

"Maybe we learned something, too," Glory said. "Now you just rest. We'll get you a nice cup of baby blue tea."

"I'll brew it!" Sparkle said eagerly.

"No, it was my idea!" Glory said. "I'll do it!"

"I want to!" Helios rushed to the kettle. "I can make a perfect cup."

The arguing went on and on. But Fira didn't hear a thing. She was fast asleep.

Join Tinker Bell, Prilla and all
the other Never Fairies in
the next Disney Fairies book...

Prilla and the
Butterfly Lie

Here is a fairy-sized preview
of the first chapter!

Prilla
and the
Butterfly
Lie

PRILLA KNELT ON the library shelf. She put her hands over her mouth to hold back her laughter. She kept her eyes on a little girl in pigtails who stood on her tiptoes, reaching for a book.

The girl grabbed the book and slid it off the shelf. Quick as a wink, Prilla popped out from the space where the book had been. The little girl stared at Prilla for a moment. Then she squealed with delight, her blue eyes wide.

"A fairy!"

"Shhh!" said the librarian. She gave the girl a stern look. Prilla giggled. She turned a somersault in the air and...

"Grab him, Prilla!" a voice cried.

Suddenly, Prilla was in a sunny meadow, back in Pixie Hollow. Nettle, a caterpillar-shearing-talent fairy, stood in front of her, holding a pair of shears. Nettle pointed to the caterpillar that Prilla was supposed to be keeping still. The caterpillar was bucking around like a little green bronco. It had knocked over a sack of caterpillar fuzz. Prilla was ankle-deep in the stuff.

Prilla sighed. It had been a long and trying day. She was very fond of Nettle, who enjoyed games as much as she did.

Just the week before, Prilla and Nettle had had a cartwheel race across a field of buttercups. Afterward, they had collapsed in the grass in a fit of giggles. That was when Nettle had asked her if she would like to give caterpillar shearing a try. Prilla had agreed.

The day had started well enough. Nettle gave Prilla a tour of the caterpillar corral. First they had seen some caterpillars hatching from eggs. Then they'd watched a few caterpillars shedding their skin. Next they had seen some furry caterpillars making their cocoons.

Suddenly, Nettle had grabbed Prilla's arm. "We're just in time to watch a butterfly hatch!" she'd whispered.

Prilla had held her breath as they'd silently watched the butterfly emerge from its cocoon. She was amazed that a funny-looking caterpillar could transform into such a beautiful creature.

Watching the butterfly hatch had been exciting. But Prilla had quickly realised that shearing caterpillars was not. Her job was to hold the caterpillars while Nettle clipped their fuzz with her shears. Prilla tried hard to help. But the truth was that she didn't really like shearing caterpillars at all. It was hot in the sun. It was dull doing the same thing over and over again. But most of all, Prilla just didn't like caterpillars. Not one bit. They were prickly. They were kind of ugly. And they were ornery.

Bored, Prilla had finally allowed herself to drift off and blink over to the mainland. Prilla was a mainland-visiting clapping-talent fairy, the only one in Pixie Hollow. In the blink of an eye, she could zip from Never Land to the mainland to visit children. Prilla's talent was very important, for it kept children's belief in fairies alive. When children didn't believe in them, fairies died.

But Prilla didn't visit the mainland only to save fairies' lives. She also went because it was her favourite thing in the world to do.

And look what had happened! She hadn't been paying attention, and now things were getting out of control.

Prilla leaned forward to grab the cranky caterpillar around its middle. It wiggled away from her, and Prilla stumbled. The other shearing-talent fairies chuckled in sympathy.

"He's a wild one, he is," said Jason, a caterpillar-shearing-talent sparrow man.

Prilla tried once again to seize the creature. The caterpillar reared up. Prilla lost her balance and fell backward. She landed in the grass with a soft thump.

"Don't worry, Prilla. You can do it!" Jason called, noticing the frown on Prilla's face.

Still the restless caterpillar wiggled. "There, there," said Nettle in a soothing voice. She put down her shears.

Nettle's gentle tone calmed the caterpillar. It began to settle down. Prilla stood and brushed herself off. Not knowing what else to do, she bent to pat the caterpillar on the head.

Quickly, Nettle began to shear the caterpillar. In a couple of minutes, she was done. "That wasn't so bad, was it?" she asked.

Prilla wasn't sure if Nettle was talking to her or to the caterpillar. She shook her head anyway.

Nettle let the newly shorn caterpillar go. Prilla watched as it inched away as fast as it could – which was pretty slow.

Nettle smiled at Prilla. "You sit and rest," she said. "I'll do the cleaning up."

Prilla lowered herself onto a moss-covered stone. She picked a stray piece of caterpillar fuzz from the hem of her pale pink silk skirt. Nettle and the other caterpillar shearers began sweeping up the loose fuzz.

Thank goodness that's over, Prilla thought. *Maybe tomorrow I won't do anything but blink over to the mainland as many times as I want.* It would be a perfect day.

Nettle put the caterpillar fuzz she'd swept up into a sack made of woven grass. She tied it shut with a flourish. Then she loaded it onto a wheelbarrow full of sacks.

Jason picked up the handles of the wheelbarrow. He set off with the load toward the Home Tree, the towering maple tree where the fairies lived and worked. "Have fun, Prilla. Thanks for your help!" he cried.

"Fly safely, Jason!" said Prilla. She waved.

Nettle sat next to her on the stone and patted Prilla's knee. "What a great day," Nettle said. "I could tell how much you enjoyed it."

"Well, I – " Prilla began.

"Being outside, working with those wonderful caterpillars." Nettle leaned in close to Prilla. She lowered her voice as if she were about to tell her a secret. "Other talents might argue with me, but caterpillar shearing really is the most important talent. Wouldn't you agree?"

She went on, not waiting for Prilla to answer. "First of all, it helps the caterpillars grow nice woolly coats for when it's time to build their cocoons. And then there're all the great things we make out of the fuzz!" She began to list them on her fingers. "Soft pillows, cosy comforters, light-as-a-feather blankets, thick sweaters, those wonderful linens… " Her voice trailed off.

Prilla nodded. She liked pillows,

comforters, blankets, sweaters, and linens as much as the next fairy did. It seemed that caterpillar shearing was indeed very important.

"Yes, it is a lovely talent," she said out loud. *I just hope I never have to help shear another caterpillar ever again!* she silently added. She leaned back on her elbows.

And before Prilla knew it, she had blinked over to the mainland. She saw a little girl holding a fluffy white dandelion. The girl pursed her lips to blow the seeds. Prilla flew toward her…

"I said, what do you think?" Nettle said suddenly.

Prilla started. Nettle was looking at her expectantly.

"Sorry, can you repeat that?"